# Bonsai for Beginners

Your Daily Guide for Bonsai Tree Care, Selection, Growing, Tools and Fundamental Bonsai Basics

**_Taisuke Ooshima, John Stallings_**

First Printing, 2013

Printed in the United States of America

*Bonsai trees represent harmony in nature - contained. They are perfect for anybody who appreciates their understated beauty and unique form.*

# Bonsai for Beginners

Your Daily Guide for Bonsai Tree Care, Selection, Growing, Tools and Fundamental Bonsai Basics

# Table of Contents

# Introduction

The thought of growing miniature trees in your garden is both challenging and exciting. It may be a lot of hard work, but it's a lot of fun as well. The best part is, the uniqueness of bonsai trees can instantly add charm to any room or garden.

Bonsai is a Japanese word that refers to the Chinese art form of growing miniature trees. In Chinese it is known as Pen-Jing, which means tray scenery. It is also sometimes known as potted scenery, trade landscape or potted landscape. Over the years, this art form has been developed to include shaping and pruning the small trees in such a manner that they will not only have a beautiful appearance, but will also provide the illusion of being older they really are. Many people prefer to create the landscape within a relatively small area and by using special trays and pots that can then be place in wooden stands that are intricately carved.

Anyone, even children, can develop growing bonsai as a hobby. Growing bonsai trees provides the distinct pleasure of being able to watch the plants as they grow based on the artistic design and shape that are given to each plant. This hobby is also quite enjoyable and relaxing, while adding beauty to the environment they inhabit.

There are different methods for growing bonsai, many of which are quite simple and require on interest and a sense of beauty. In order to successful grow and cultivate bonsai, there are a few basic things you will need to know, including how to get started growing bonsai and how to properly care for your plants.

In this guide we will cover everything you need to know to begin growing bonsai, the different ways that bonsai can be grown, how to care for and develop your plants and even the various types of plants that can be used for growing bonsai.

Once you have tried growing bonsai for the first time, you may just find that it becomes a hobby you will never tire of.

So, are you ready to learn the exciting and enjoyable hobby of growing bonsai? Whether you have a green thumb or not, bonsai trees will definitely win you over.

# The Ultimate Bonsai Starting Guide

Before we begin, we must first discuss a few important points about bonsai trees. Look at this chapter as an introductory kit - here we will learn the history and origin of bonsai trees, the initial tools you'll be needing and of couse, the basic bonsai tree varieties you will be choosing from to grow your very first bonsai tree.

Sinces bonsai trees aren't justregular types of trees, they require special care and attention to be able to successfully grow and appreciate them. Several introductory elements must be learned to have a deeper understanding of how bonsai trees are best grown and cared for.

# Bonsai Plants: Where did they come from?

Although bonsai trees are commonly thought of as being just strictly Japanese, the history of this art form is actually a blend of many different cultures. The first time bonsai appeared was in China more than one thousand years ago. Originally, it was known as 'pun-sai', which was the act of growing single trees on pots. Some of the earliest versions of 'pun-sai' resembled animals; often forming the figures of birds and dragons.

These trees were extremely expensive and were primarily purchase by only the elite in China. Plants that are shaped like serpents and fiery dragons can also be found in these early versions on bonsai.

It was when Japan began to adopt the Chinese culture that it also began to dabble in the art of bonsai. Bonsai was first introduced in Japan during the Kamakura period, between 1185 and 1333 A.D. Bonsai was introduced to Japan by Zen Buddhists, a religion which was rapidly spreading across all of Asia at that time.

The art form of bonsai became polished once it was introduced to Japan. It quickly became symbolic of the elite in Japanese society, even though it had originally been introduced by monks. Bonsai is said to represent the harmony that exists between the soul of man and nature. During the 17th and 18th centuries, bonsai reached even greater heights, as Japanese art forms reached their peak.

The art form on bonsai began to evolve once more when Japanese philosophy was melded with it. As a result, all of the parts of the plant, with the exception of the body were removed. It was through this transition that bonsai became more accessible to the Japanese public as a whole.

Cultural elements such as accent plants and rocks were then introduced. Even small buildings and people began to appear. This art form was known as bon-kei. The art form of reproducing miniature landscapes within nature is known as sai-kei.

During the mid-19th century, Japan became open to the rest of the world and subsequently bonsai became popular around the world. It was during the Paris World Exhibition in 1900 that the eyes of the world were first introduced to the small trees. Later exhibitions taking place in Vienna and London make bonsai even more popular.

Over time, bonsai has become symbolic of the culture and ideals of Japan. Even now in modern times, the New Year would not be complete without the 'tonkonama.' This is where the Japanese traditionally display their gifts and includes the bonsai of an apricot or plum tree.

# It's All about Your Tool Kit

Growing bonsai is actually not as difficult as you might imagine it to be, but it is important that you have the right tools on hand. Bonsai creation is most definitely an art form and like any art form, you must have the proper tools.

Clipping, pruning, wiring and training are all necessary in order to create a bonsai tree and maintain its unique form. The special tools that are necessary to train and shape a bonsai tree can typically be purchased from your local hardware store or from a gardening store. Below is a guide to the tools you will need to successful grow bonsai.

## Scissors

Scissors are an absolutely necessity for the purpose of pruning and clipping the branches, leaves and roots of your bonsai tree.

Scissors can be made from a wide variety of different metals and can also come in many different shapes and sizes.

There can also be different degrees of sharpness from one pair of scissors to another, as well as quality. Make a point to choose a pair of scissors that are very sharp.

Also, they need to be of a size that will allow you to reach the most difficult to access parts of the bonsai tree. Look for a pair of scissors made of stainless steel.

## Shaping Knife

You will also need a shaping knife. These knives are very sharp and the edges have a concave shape. They make it much easier to shape your bonsai plant. Look for a shaping knife that is razor sharp and has a good quality.

## Tool Kit

In addition, you will need a tool kit. It can be quite difficult to dig through the soil using your hands in a miniature bonsai pot. A tool kit makes the job much easier.

A tool kit contains a small plower that makes it easier for turning and lightly plowing the soil mixture. Look for tools made of steel, as they are more durable. A tool kit should also contain copper wires along with wire cutters.

Along with the tools mentioned above, you will also need to have a sense of artistry as well as patience and meticulousness. Growing bonsai does require some skill, but that is something you can gain with practice.

# Bonsai Varieties: Which One Will You Start With?

One thing to keep in mind is that there are special types of tree varieties that are commonly used more frequently in growing bonsai. There are both indoor as well as outdoor varieties you can consider. Some of the more common indoor varieties include:

- Boxwood

- Gardenia

- Serissa

- Norfolk islands pine

- Azalea

- Aralia

- Ficus

Each of these plants have a wooden stem and tend to work well with wiring, meaning it can be fairly easy to wire the branches and roots of these plants and train them to grow in the desired direction.

You should always keep in mind that you select tropical or subtropical plants, you will need to make certain the temperature does not fall below 50 degrees. Also, tropical plants should never be left under harsh sunlight. Instead, sunlight should be filtered through a glass window.

You will likely find that the choices for indoor bonsai plants are somewhat limited. There are far more options to choose from when it comes to outdoor bonsai plants. Some popular options that are suitable for outdoor bonsai plants include:

- Flowering crab apple

- Hawthorn

- Ginkgo biloba

- Pines and their sub varieties

- Elms and their sub varieties

- Maples and their sub varieties

- Junipers

Other trees you might consider for bonsai growing include:

- Judas tree

- Hackberry

- Horse chestnut

- Hazel trees and their sub varieties

- JadesSmoke tree

Once you have your tools ready and you know from which tree variety you'd like to start with then congratulations, you are one step ahead and almost there to begin growing your first bonsai!

# Small But Incredible: Types of Bonsai Trees

Apart from the tree varieties mentioned in the previous chapter, there are also different bonsai tree typesto select from.

Bonsai trees are all about beauty and uniqueness. In order to enjoy your first bonsai experience to the fullest, you must start with a bonsai type that suits your personal taste.

Research is paramount at this point so to help narrow down your choices, here are the different types of bonsai trees.

# Which type suits your taste?

## Bald Cypress

Although it grows very slowly, the Bald Cypress is one of the most popular types of bonsai trees. It is known for its light, feathery foliage and the orangey-brown color it attains in the fall. This tree can be grown in many different types of soil, including those that are well-drained.

The Bald Cypress can be successful grown in Europe as well as Asia. This plant does require climates with hot summers. If planted in areas where the summers are cool; it will grow but at a slower rate. The Bald Cypress is an excellent tree for those new to growing bonsai because it grows so easily.

## Okinawa Holly

The Okinawa Holly is a smaller version of the Holly that is known for producing small pink flowers during the spring and summer. It is native to the Northern Hemisphere.

This plant is particularly known for its hardiness as well as its unique appearance, making it ideal for bonsai. Due to the fact that it is easy to care for, it is perfect for beginners.

You can usually expect this plant to reach about six inches in height by the age of four.

## Snowbush

This plant is also known as Snow on the Mountain. Known for its large leaf size and fantastic color, which often depends on the lighting, it is a popular plant. This plant will reach around seven inches in height by around age four.

## Shimpaku

This plant is also known as the Chinese Juniper. It is a wonderful choice for bonsai because it is very tolerant of different types of soils. Interestingly, there are both male and female plants of these species. The Shimpaku is naturally irregularly shaped and grows in a type of mound shape. This plant features round foliage with needs that are dark green.

## Lavender Star Flower

This plant is a somewhat compact evergreen tree. It is original to Africa and Australia. In total, there are more than 400 different species of this plant around the world. The flowers produced have a beautiful lavender color. By around age ten, this plant will reach approximately ten inches in height.

## Dwarf Pomegranate

This plant is a type of subtropical deciduous tree that produces trumpet shaped flowers and small ornamental fruit. While the flowers and fruit are an orange-red color, the leaves are dark with slight bronze hues. The Dwarf Pomegranate is native to the Mediterranean and Asia.

Consequently it requires warmer temperatures in order for the fruit to open.

## Flowering Crabapple

This plant is one of the best types of flowering trees for bonsai. It is known for producing brilliant white flowers with a wonderful fragrance. The flowers begin to color the tree during the early spring months, just prior to foliage. Once the foliage on this plant has begun to grow you are likely to notice small green growths that resemble small apples. The crabapples will continue to ripen with a variety of colors throughout the fall months. This plant is very easy to grow as well as maintain, making it a good choice for beginners.

## Jaboticaba

This plant is native to Brazil and is a member of the Myrtle family. It is similar to the Guava plant. Along with producing flowers, the Jaboticaba plant also produces fruit once it is mature.

## Chinese Bird Plum

A beautiful flowering tree, the Chinese Bird Plum is a type of semitropical evergreen tree. Native to Asia as well as some parts of North America, this plant is also grown through China.

One of the most interesting facts about this plant is that while it will remain an evergreen when it is grown in mild climates, when grown in temperate regions it becomes deciduous.

## Bamboo

There are many different types of bamboo that can be grown for bonsai. One of the most popular is the Lucky Bamboo, also known as the Lotus Bamboo. You also have a variety of different choices regarding how you want to grow bamboo as bonsai. For instance, you can choose to grow a single stalk or if you prefer you can bundle up several stalks and display them.

## Holly

There are more than 400 different species of Holly, which is deciduous and part of the evergreen family. Some types of Holly are shrubs while others are climbers. They come from all parts of the world, including some regions that are tropical and subtropical. There are both male and female flowers.

## Ponytail Palm

The Ponytail Palm is one of the most unique types of trees for growing bonsai. The most interesting aspect of this plant is the rather swollen base of the tree. In addition the texture of the trunk both feels and looks like the foot of an elephant. This is why this plant is also sometimes known as Elephant's Foot. The trunk of the plant is used for storing water that can be used during dry times. This tree is capable of holding enough water when grown in the wild that it can survive for four weeks without water.

## Brush Cherry

This plant is also known as the Syzygium Paniculatum. You will notice that the leaves on this plant are small and firm and have a glossy appearance. It produces puffy white flowers. When given sufficient light, it is also known for developing red highlights within the leaves. By age ten, this plant usually reaches about 14 inches in height.

## Ginkgo

Native to Japan, this plant is capable of living up to 100 years. It is also known as a highly revered tree in Japan. Although it is commonly associated with health foods, this tree is ideal for growing bonsai.

## Hawaiian Umbrella Tree

The dwarf version of this tree is perfect for growing bonsai. This is often one of the easiest trees to grow as well as maintain, which makes it ideal for beginners. It is known for being able to handle low light conditions, which also makes it good for indoor growth.

## Hinoki Cypress

This plant is also known as the False Cypress. It is an evergreen conifer that features deep green, flat foliage that fans out. One of the most interesting aspects of this plant is that the edges of the leaves feature a blue hue.

When mature, this plant will produce small cones that are usually about the size of a pea.

## Japanese White Pine

This plant is known for its striking beauty when grown into a bonsai. Although it is dense, it can grow up to a height of fifty feet in the wild. Naturally irregularly shaped, it features a beautiful and broad spread. The needles of the Japanese White Pine are twisted and have blue-green tufts.

## Fukien Tea

This plant is native to southeast China. An evergreen, it is named for the Fuijan province. The leaves on this tree are dark green, small and shiny. They feature small hairs. When still young, this plant has light brown bark that will begin to crack as it matures. During the early summer months, small flowers are produced that later turn into small black berries.

## Boxwood

This tree falls into the evergreen shrub category, of which there are about 70 different types.

It is commonly found in rocky hill areas in Asia, Africa, Europe and Central America.

During the spring, this plant displays yellow male flowers that are surrounded by small female flowers.

## Trident Maple

This plant is kin to the Japanese Maple plant and is known for being ideal for growing bonsai. During the fall it features magnificent colors that range from faded orange to deep red.

## Zelkova

There are actually many different types of Zelkova that are excellent for growing bonsai. The Elm Zelkova and the Japanese Zelkova are two of the most popular choices. These plants are native to Western Asia and prefer cooler climates.

## Wisteria

This plant is known for its twining and climbing and is primarily grown in moist areas in Japan, China and Korea as well as the southern and central regions of the United States.

Features beautiful green leaves and magnificent flowers, this tree is a favorite for bonsai enthusiasts.

## Magnolia

There are different types of magnolia that can be grown for bonsai, but the Star is considered to be one of the best. It is a slow growing shrub that is typically dense and bushy. It can take up to thirty years for this plant to produce flowers.

Once it does begin to display flowers, they are white and star-shaped.

## Azalea

The Satsuki Azalea is one of the most popular choices for growing bonsai. This plant is extremely hardy and produces beautiful flowers that can reach up to seven inches in diameter.

## Juniper

Juniper is one of the hardiest conifers. It is non-flowering and is excellent for bonsai growing due to the fact that it is so easy to prune and train. It features fast growth patterns with branches that are long and flowing and can be trained in practically any style of bonsai.

## Japanese Maple

This plant is most commonly grown in gardens. It is excellent for growing bonsai because it is extremely compact, but features delicate foliage. In the fall it produces magnificent red and gold foliage. There are more than 300 different species that vary in terms of leaf shape, color and size.

## Japanese Black Pine

This tree is considered to be one of the best for growing bonsai. It is quite strong and is known for responding well to a variety of different techniques.

Due to the fact that this tree is so versatile and hardy, it is ideal for novices as well as advanced bonsai growers.

## Flowering Quince

This plant is another wonderful choice for growing bonsai. During the winter it will produce beautiful white and red flowers on twisted bare branches. It is native to numerous countries in Asia, including Japan, Korea and China. This plant is frost hardy and is capable of adapting to a variety of different environments.

## Camellia

There are many different species of this plant, more than 250 in all. The most popular choice is the Camellia sasanqua. This variety is known for being small and hardy. There is a disadvantage to this type of plant, which is that it can be susceptible to frost. The leaves on this plant are typically large and glossy, ranging from medium to dark green.

## Jade Tree

This plant is native to South Africa.

An evergreen, it is best to grow this plant inside and assure that it is not exposed to temperatures below 41 degrees. The leaves on this plant are known for turning red at the edges when provided with sufficient sunlight. The tree also produces lovely star-shaped blossoms during the fall.

## Fuchsia

There are more than 8,000 different types of Fuchsia.

The most important thing to keep in mind when selecting a Fuchsia plant is that while you can maintain control over the density and size of the leaf growth on this plan, the flowering size cannot be controlled. As a result, it is important to only choose those types of plants for bonsai that produce small flowers.

Some of the best choices include F. Lady Thumb, Microphylla and F Tom Thumb.

## Ficus

This is a deciduous tree that is native to Southeast Asia. There are hundreds of different types of species.

## Dwarf Pomegranate

This is a subtropical deciduous tree that makes an excellent choice for growing bonsai due to its flowering and fruiting abilities. One of the most interesting aspects of this plant is that each aspect of the plant is the same as the tree when fully grown. For example, the flowers, fruits and leaves are all the same with the exception that they are miniaturized.

## Cotoneaster

This is a deciduous shrub that is both hardy and easy to grown. It makes a wonderful choice for bonsai, especially for beginners. The leaves tend to be small, while the tree produces flowers that are delicate and lovely during the spring.

## Chinese Elm

This is by far one of the most popular types of trees for growing bonsai. In the wild, this tree can easily reach heights of up to sixty feet. This plant can also quite easily be trained for perfect bonsai growing.

Take into consideration which types of bonsai trees are ideal for beginnes. Once you've learned the ropes of growing bonsai trees, you can choose from some of the more complicated types.

# How To Select Your First Bonsai

Now that you have knowledge about the different types and varieties of bonsai plants, you are now ready to choose your first actual bonsai.

In this chapter, we will be discussing tips on selecting your first bonsai, choosing the right pot for your plant, some special starting techniques and different methods to help you get started.

Now, the first most important step is to choose the right tree and to learn how to specifically cultivate and grow that tree.Once you've learned this, everything else will come easier.

## The Nursery Is Best for Beginners

If you are a beginner and you would like to get started cultivating bonsai trees with a sapling there are a couple of different options that are available to you. You can choose a sapling from a local nursery or you can select one from a nearby forested area.

If you are a complete beginner to growing bonsai, keep in mind that the best option is typically to select a bonsai from a nursery. The advantage to this is that the nursery can assist you in determining the most suitable tree. Always remember that not all trees can be grown into bonsai plants. The nursery will be able to provide guidance to you in determining which type of tree will be most suitable for your purposes.

You must also remember to keep seasonal changes in mind when choosing a tree. This will help you in understanding the requirements of the tree at a later date. This is why selecting a sapling from the natural environment can often prove to be difficult. You cannot be absolutely certain of the type of tree you are getting.

Many people choose to purchase a bonsai starter kit when they are first getting started with growing bonsai trees. These types of kits are typically inexpensive and are ideal for beginners. They will contain a bonsai sapling as well as an instruction guide relating to that sapling and all of the crucial steps that must be followed in order to grow a bonsai tree. In addition, the kit will usually include bonsai pots and pruning tools.

## The Right Pot Makes All the Difference

Along with selecting the right sapling you must also know how to choose the right pot for your bonsai tree. Even if your sapling is already in a pot, keep in mind that at some point you will need to transplant it. There are several important points that should be kept in mind whenever you need to pot or repot a bonsai tree.

- The depth, width and length of the pot must be taken into consideration as they must be sufficient enough to hold water and soil for the healthy growth of the tree. Size is extremely important as the pot is usually smaller than the tree and yet it must be able to hold all of the important nutrients the plant needs.

- The pot must be capable of supporting the tree for a long time. The material the pot is made of must be durable and strong enough to easily withstand the pressure of the water and the soil. This is why many bonsai pots have wide bases.

- In terms of proportion, it is imperative to strike a healthy balance between the tree and the plant.

- Remember that the pot will need to be replaced as the tree grows in size and begins to take shape.

# Start It Right!

## Trained Bonsai

For those who are impatient and wish to get started right away with their bonsai tree, the best method is often to purchase a bonsai tree that has already been trained. This will help to save time and effort, especially if you are a beginner. You can frequently find bonsai trees that are either partially trained or fully trained in many nurseries and garden center. They can also be ordered online.

What makes these trees ideal is that they have been cultivated by professionals and experts who have spent years honing their skills and cultivating bonsais from seeds or seedlings. You should expect that these types of trees are usually going to be expensive, given the amount of time and effort that have been spent cultivating them.

Although these trees may have been partially trained, you still gain the advantage of being able to shape the tree according to your own desires. Even with a bonsai tree that has been fully trained, it is still possible to make modifications, even if they are somewhat limited. The advantage of a bonsai tree that has been fully trained is that you can begin enjoying it in its fully glory immediately.

## Using Wild Plants

Practically any type of plant can be used to grow a bonsai tree. Even so, it can take quite a bit of effort and time to cultivate even a single bonsai tree. In some cases, there can be errors made along the way that cannot be repaired.

To avoid these types of problems, it is important to learn how to properly inspect a plant before considering it for a possible bonsai project. The following guidelines should be utilized whenever you are collecting wild specimens as well as when you are shopping in a garden center or nursery to attain the best results.

## Roots

The best plants are those that do not need a lot of work in regards to the roots. This is because it can take a lot of time and effort to correct the root spread, or Nebari, of a bonsai tree. Whenever you plan to cultivate traditional bonsai forms, it is important to avoid plans that have a root system that is slanting, or Shakan, or those with group planting, also known as Yose-ue. As a general rule of thumb, if the root spread of a plant goes evenly in all directions, that plant is a suitable candidate for a bonsai.

## The Trunk

Immature trees within thin trunks can typically be pruned into the shape y desire. This is not the case with a mature tree that has a thick trunk. Always keep this in mind when choose a plant.

For traditional bonsai forms, remember that the tree of the tree will narrow as it grows upward. This is known as Kokejun or tapering. In addition, the tree is usually a good choice if the initial rise, or Tachiagari, sufficiently displays the unique characteristics of the tree. This is the area located between the root system and the first branch or Ichi-no-eda.

Make it a point to stay away from trees that have trunks with parts that swell. Also, you should steer away from trees with trunks that are injured. This is because it can take them a long time to fully heal and there may still be permanent scars.

## The Branches

Pruning branches can be relatively easy. Always remember that new branches will not grow as you expect them. This process also takes time. If there are numerous branches on the tree, it provides more room and flexibility for creativity and you have a better opportunity of being able to cultivate the tree however you wish. Consequently, it is a good idea to select a tree that has a lot of branches.

## The Leaves

In plants, the quality of the leaves is typically a hereditary matter. If you dislike certain characteristics, stay away from trees that have those characteristics.

## Pests and Diseases

It is always important to inspect the tree to determine whether it might have any infestations or diseases. Yellow leaves during the wrong season as well as abnormalities that appear on the bark can both be indications of a pest infestation. Look for trees with healthy bark and leaves.

# The Learning Curve: Methods for Beginners

There are many different methods you can learn and use for getting started, based on your experience and level of interest.

## Air Layering

Air layering is a type of method that is used for growing trees by removing a large branch or a section of the trunk in order to create an entirely new tree. One of the primary benefits of growing bonsai trees through the air layering method is that you are able to establish a fairly sizeable tree within a single growing season. All of the other methods, with the exception of collecting, require several seasons for full development.

While the process of air layering may seem difficult at first, it is actually not that challenging once you have a solid understanding of the steps involved.

1. Remember that the best time to get started is between the time in spring when the tree buds and the time in summer when the growth of the tree is most active.

2. The best place on the tree to remove the bark is at the node. This is the place located below the spot where the branch and the trunk separate and where the leaves begin growing. This is the place where the roots grow most easily.

3. The first step is to cut the upper side of the skinned portion, right where the roots grow. Cut it into a sawtooth shape. This will allow the roots to grow more evenly.

4. In order to grow the roots, you must ensure the pruned parts are kept moist. The best method for doing this is to wrap the parts that have been skinned with soil, moss or some other type of material that can retain moisture.

## Working with Cuttings

The advantage of working with cuttings is that this method allows you the ability to create multiple trees that are nearly identical to the original tree. If you like the characteristics of the original tree and want to replicate them in new trees, this is an excellent way to do so. Starting bonsai trees from cuttings also goes faster than starting from seeds. In some cases, you may even be able to save yourself weeks.

The cuttings method involves cutting branches from a tree and then transplanting them into soil for the purpose of producing new trees. This method is most commonly used for growing very high quality material for cultivating bonsai trees. Another advantage to this method is that it is possible to make a twin-trunk, Sokan, or triple trunk, Sankan, bonsai tree by inserting two or three pronged branches into the soil.

Of course, keep in mind that if the new roots do not develop properly or if the branch is not inserted into the soil at the right angle, it makes it almost impossible for the lower portion of the trunk to grow properly. This method is most efficient if you use the actively growing branches that you prune from the original tree.

As a general rule of thumb, the best time to take cuttings is during the spring time. This is when the growth of the tree becomes active gradually. Taking a cutting is extremely easy. You just need a pruned branch and then insert it into the soil. The most important thing is whether the roots will grow outward once you have transplanted the branch. Keep the following guidelines in mind for optimal growth.

1. Always make sure you use new soil. Be sure to rinse the soil carefully so that it doesn't contain anything organic that might make the plant more susceptible to rotting.

2. Water the soil in advance and allow the water to permeate the soil completely. Allow it to sit for awhile before you attempt to insert the branch.

3. When taking a cutting, be sure to cut the branch using a pair of sharp scissors. This will ensure the cross section is completely smooth. In addition, make sure you use an oblique cut to ensure a larger cross-section area. You can also make two cuts so that the cross sections will form a V.

4. At the same time, you might consider pruning the leaves in order to reduce their mass. This is because the branch will absorb less water once it is transplanted into the soil.

5. Finally, soak the pruned branch in water at least thirty minutes to allow it to absorb a sufficient amount of water. This is because the branch may not be able to absorb enough water once it has been transplanted.

## Growing from Seeds

Growing your bonsai trees from seeds has two advantages. First, you have the benefit of being able to grow species of trees that are rare for a relatively small price. You can typically purchase a package of bonsai seeds for less than five dollars.

Second, once you have successfully germinated your seeds and started growing your trees, you can have complete control over every aspect of the growth of the tree throughout each stage of development. This means you have the opportunity to be able to raise a very high quality bonsai tree.

The style as well as the shape and size of the bonsai tree will be completely under your control right from the very beginning.

Remember that it can take between three to four years to grow Zelkova trees from seeds and up to five years to grow Hackberries. No matter what type of species you decide upon, always make sure you soak your seeds overnight before sowing them.

## Grafting

The grafting method is usually only used when it is not possible to use the cutting or seed methods. Through the grafting method it is possible to take a section of the desired original plant and attach it to a transplanted tree, known as the rootstock. Many nurseries frequently used the grafting technique to reproduce desirable species of plants.

Keep in mind that the rootstock tree should be the same species as the parent tree for successful grafting.

# The Best Grafting Techniques

Grafting techniques can commonly be used to reproduce large amounts of desirable plants. Some of the most desirable characteristics for bonsai plants include:

- Form

- Color

- Branch and trunk structure

- Bark texture

- Range of leaf shapes

- Sizes

- Textures

- Range of needle shape, sizes and textures

Keep in mind that grafting is often the most expensive method. This is because grafting can be a challenge that takes years, based on the species. Sometimes only a small percentage of grafts will actually take. It also helps to have a solid understanding of the many different types of grafting techniques as well as a sense of artistry.

Don't worry if you don't get it right the first time. Even the experts took years to master these techniques. Remember, practice and patience are what will get you there.

# How to Care for Your Bonsai the Right Way

Now we've arrived at the most challenging yet most enjoyable part of the process– taking care of your bonsai. Like any other plant, bonsai trees require constant TLC. Successfully growing your first bonsai is one thing, but keeping it alive and healthy is what matters.

# Initial Tips on Taking Care of Your Bonsai Plant

A bonsai should be regularly fed, watered and groomed to be able to grow properly. In this chapter, we will discuss all of these important points plus some helpful tips on how to properly care for your new plant.

Here are a few initial tips on how you can maintain your bonsai successfully:

## Keep It Hydrated

Water is essential to survival of your bonsai tree. The amount of water your plant will need will depend upon its environment, but it will need regular watering. Without a sufficient amount of water it will be impossible for your tree to prosper and it could die. At the same time, keep in mind that you should not over-water your plant.

The best way to water your plant is with a water sprinkler or with a spritz spray. Remember to spray from the sides and from the top so that you wet the leaves. You will know you have watered it enough when the soil is moist and the leaves are wet.

Simply pouring water at the roots of the plant will do nothing but wash away the soil and the fertilizers. This type of method for watering can also cause damage to the root system, which is already fragile. This can make your plant more susceptible to rot. Remember that tray or pot should have a hole at the bottom so that excess water can drain away.

Keep in mind that you should never allow the soil in your bonsai tree to become dry. You should water whenever the soil appears to be somewhat dry. If your bonsai tree is receiving full sunlight you may need to water it once per day. The amount of watering your plant needs may depend upon the environment as well as the type of tree you have, the type of soil used and the size of your pot.

Take the time to carefully evaluate the watering requirements of your bonsai tree and then adjust your watering schedule. You may also find it to be a good idea to use a moisture meter until you have developed a good idea of the watering requirements of your tree.

## Keep It Humid

Throughout the winter months when your bonsai tree is inside you should place it in a shallow tray that has been filled with a layer of gravel and some water. This will help to provide additional moisture around the tree, which is important as water tends to evaporate and can reduce the amount of moisture that is lost due to interior heating systems.

## Keep It Fertilized

Fertilizing is important to ensure your bonsai tree remains healthy. Due to the fact that your bonsai tree is being grown in a relatively small amount of soil it will be necessary to replenish the supply of nutrients in the soil from time to time. You can use any type of general purpose liquid fertilizer, which you should be able to readily find at a garden center. The best way to use fertilizer is at half its recommended strength. Apply fertilizer once per month with one exception: during the winter months.

## Keep It in the Right Temperature

Keep in mind that not all trees are created equal. Depending on the tree species, the temperature for optimum growth is between 20 degrees Celsius (68°Fahrenheit) and 30 degrees Celsius (86° Fahrenheit). 45 degrees Celsius (113 F) is the upper temperature limit of trees but this is dependent on different factors such as the tree's ability to adjust to temperature, the duration of its exposure to hot temperatures, its water content and the age of its tissues.

The usual temperature of a tree is slightly above the ambient room temperature. If your bonsai has sufficient soil moisture, it will increase its ability to fight off enormous heat loads. We'll discuss more of this in the summer and winter care section of this book.

# Watering Your Bonsai Plant

If you get thirsty from time to time, so does your bonsai. Keep in mind that water is a plant's lifeline – dehydration is the number one cause of death in bonsai plants. Many experts believe that watering is the most important part of bonsai care.

A regular watering schedule for your plant is crucial, provided that you are already familiar with your particular bonsai's needs. One effective way to get on that schedule is to place your bonsai in a location where you won't forget to water it. You can tell that your bonsai is thirsty by feeling its soil. If it feels dry, it means that your plant needs some watering. Another easy way to do this is to simply pick up the plant – thirsty plants will feel lighter than well-watered ones.

## How Often and How Much?

"How often should I water my bonsai?" is one of the most frequently asked questions when it comes to bonsai care. The simple answer is that bonsai plants need to be watered at least once a day. This, though, depends on many variables such as the type of tree, the time of year, where you keep your tree and where you live. Early in the morning is the best time to water your bonsai, before they start their photosynthetic activities.

How much water you should give your plant also depends on a variety of factors. The amount of water that trees use is influenced by temperature, humidity and wind. The kind of potting mixture used also affects your plant's water usage because elements in some potting mixtures hold more water than others.

## Misting

Misting, or *Hamisu* in Japanese is basically light topical watering during summer days. Misting refreshes the bonsai by wetting the whole tree – the foliage, the trunk, the soil and even the pot. Mist your bonsai once or twice in a day following your early morning watering. Light watering is most effective in the late afternoon when the sun is about to set.

## Watering Tips

- Only use room temperature tap water for watering your bonsai. Cold water may shock its roots.

- When watering bonsai, water the whole plant, not just the soil. All parts of a plant absorb water and about 35% of its water intake doesn't involve the roots.

- Wet the soil a little first to increase its ability to absorb a larger volume of water, then water thoroughly until the soil is saturated.

- Be sure that your pot has working drainage holes at the bottom.

- During the first few weeks, regularly check the soil of your bonsai to determine your watering schedule.

# Feeding Your Bonsai Plant

Feeding or fertilizing your bonsai is yet again another important part of bonsai care. While water and sunlight are considered to be "plant food", fertilizer serves as its "vitamins". Fertilizers contain potassium, phosphorus, nitrogen and other important nutrients that your plant needs for photosynthesis, cell division and various enzyme processes. You'll want to use a 10-10-10 or 20-

20-20 fertilizer (this means that the fertilizer contains equal amounts of the three most important ingredients – nitrogen, phosphorus and potassium).

They are also used to provide an optimum amount of salt to your plant's soil. You can tell if your bonsai is receiving the correct amount of nutrition through its color – healthy plants display foliage of vibrant dark green color.

## How Often and How Much?

Like any other tree, you should only feed your bonsai during periods of active growth. This is generally from mid-spring until early summer as well as late summer through early fall. Every other week is a good period. Again, how much you should use depends on the type of bonsai you are caring for. I suggest that you use the fertilizer as directed – never feed your bonsai more or less than the recommended amount. Each fertilizer packaging usually has instructions of the right dosage to use as well as the frequency of feeding.

## Feeding Tips

- There are both solid and liquid fertilizers. Solid fertilizers are used to feed the soil while liquid fertilizers are used on the bonsai's leaves. Use an ordinary spray bottle to spray the leaves with fertilizer. Use the specified dilution in the fertilizer package.

- Use a fertilizer that is rich in nitrogen during spring months because it stimulates leaf growth.

49

- Use a fertilizer that is rich in potassium after trimming your bonsai.

- When you run out of fertilizer, purchase a new brand. Each brand contains different amounts of trace elements as well as minerals and exposing your plant to different amounts of these nutrients will benefit its growth.

- Water your bonsai thoroughly before feeding it. Never fertilize a dry plant.

# Grooming Your Bonsai Plant

Bonsai is often referred to as "plant art". It involves a variety of techniques such as pinching, trimming, pruning and wiring in order to achieve its majestic miniature tree look.

## Pinching and Trimming

In order to ensure your bonsai tree remains miniature you will need to trim it and pinch it. Trimming and pinching helps to hold back the new growth of the plant safely. Remember that you should never remove all of the new growth.

Always leave some of the new growth to help sustain the tree. If you have a tropical or sub-tropical tree you will need to pinch it and trim it from time to time throughout the year. Keep in mind that you will need to adjust your schedule based on the growth rate of your specific tree.

## Pruning

To maintain your plant as a bonsai and help in shaping it, you will need to prune it. This involves clipping and directing the new branches and roots so that you are able to train as well as stunt the natural growth of the plant. If you see a new branch appear that you do not wish to be present, you will need to prune it down to a bud.

This will make it possible for new branches to follow the same direction. Through this method you will be able to cultivate your bonsai into the shape and design you desire.

Remember that it is usually best to adhere to the natural shape that follows the full-size tree. If you attempt to experiment too much you may find that your bonsai does not flourish too well.

Evergreen bonsai trees will be able to keep their green leaves throughout the entire year. On the other hand, deciduous bonsai trees shed their leaves during the fall and winter, with new leaves growing in the spring.

Always remember that the presence of leaves that are dry and brittle and yellow is a sign that your plant is not getting enough water. Leaves that start to turn yellow and fall are a sign that you may be over-watering your bonsai.

## Wiring

Wiring is another technique used to groom your bonsai. It basically means attaching temporary wires to your bonsai to achieve a desired position. This is usually done to add to the impression of age or to simply increase your plant's artistic effect.

Wiring is one of the more complex bonsai techniques and should be learned thoroughly to successfully achieve it. It involves bending your bonsai's trunks and branches with the use of wire so you should do it with outmost care.

It is best to wire your bonsai from mid to late summer when it is in an active growth period. Remove the wires from your tree by cutting it as unwinding it may cause damage to the branches.

## Repotting

As previously mentioned, from time to time you will need to repot your bonsai tree. You will know it is time to repot your tree when the root system has filled the bonsai pot. Repotting is important to ensure your tree has fresh soil as well as to promote a more compact root system.

Generally speaking, most deciduous bonsai trees will need to be repotted every two to three years. Evergreen trees should only need to be repotted every four to five years.

Due to the fact that trees naturally grow at different rates, you may need to adjust this schedule somewhat. Be sure to examine the root system of your tree on an annual basis to determine whether you need to repot it.

The potting process is typically quite easy and safe to the plant, provided you perform it properly and making sure you do it at the right time of year. Repotting should always be performed in mid-summer. You will need to make sure you remove the tree along with all of its soil from the pot. You will also need to remove the outer and bottom quarter of the root mass of the tree. You can do this by gently raking away the soil and then pruning back the roots of the tree.

For the most part you do not need to prune back more than 1/4 of the root mass. After you have done this, you can then place the tree back into its original pot or you can put it into another pot. Make sure you place screen over the drainage holes in the pot and then a thin layer of small size gravel in the bottom of the pot. This will help with drainage.

Place a layer of fresh new soil over the gravel and then a layer of soil that drains well. This will help to elevate the tree up to its previous height in the pot.

Once you have placed the bonsai tree back into the pot you should fill the area that has been left vacant by the pruned roots with fresh soil. Be sure to work in the soil around and under the roots so that there aren't any air pockets left exposed.

You will need to thoroughly water your bonsai tree after you have repotted it. You can do this by submerging the pot in a tub of water. Finally, use moss or some other type of ground cover over the surface of the pot to help prevent the soil from becoming eroded when you water the plant.

# Protecting Your Bonsai from Pests

Due to the fact that your bonsai tree is really a tree in miniature form, you can treat it for insects and diseases in the same way you would treat any other tree.

So there is no need for special pesticides.

As soon as you notice that something might be wrong with your bonsai tree, it might be ill, leaves are falling off for no reason or any other issues, take it to a specialized store where they sell pesticides. The person there will know what it needs, and will give you the right medicine for it.

# Seasonal Maintenance

Let's face it, it won't be a perfect sunny day all year long. If seasons change, so do the needs of your bonsai. If you're already familiar with your bonsai care routine, there are just a few adjustments you will have to make during extreme hot or cold weather.

Here are some reminders for caring for your bonsai during summer and winter:

## Summer Care

If the temperatures at night do not fall below 40 degrees, your bonsai tree can be safely placed outside. Remember to position it so that it can receive a sufficient amount of sunlight, including morning sun and shade in the afternoon. Most bonsai trees are best viewed when they are positioned about three to four feet high, which is at eye level.

## Winter Care

Once the temperatures began to approach the 40 degree mark you need to bring your tree back inside. You will need to do this over a period of weeks, gradually. First, bring your plant in for a few hours at a time and then return it back outside.

Slowly increase the amount of time that your plant spends indoors so that it is able to become acclimated to the new environment. Never suddenly bring your plant inside and leave it there.

The best location for your plant indoors is on a south-facing window. If that is not available, consider a window that offers western or eastern exposure. While you can place it in a northern facing window, you will need to use grow lights to ensure your bonsai tree has enough light to remain healthy. Your bonsai tree will need between four and six hours of sunlight per day.

By properly caring for your bonsai tree you can ensure that it will remain healthy and miniature in form for your enjoyment for many years into the future. Remember that your tree should continue to increase in it beauty as it matures over the years.

While growing and cultivating a bonsai tree can sometimes appear to be somewhat of a challenge, it can also be highly rewarding. The time you spend cultivating and growing your tree as you practice and hone your skills will be well worth it in the end.

Without proper care and attention, you won't be able to enjoy the true rewards of having a bonsai plant. So be sure follow the instructions listed above to have a wonderful bonsai experience.

# Conclusions

Like I mentioned in the previous chapters, growing bonsai trees can be extremely rewarding because of its beauty and uniqueness. However, it will take time and patience to learn all the necessary steps to care for and cultivate it.

Of course, the creativity you exhibit also goes a long way in caring for bonsai plants. With these being said, growing a bonsai tree indeed is a unique experience you will never get tired of.

Whether you are completely new to cultivating bonsai trees or you have dabbled some with them in the past, there is always something new to learn about the art of bonsai.

While this guide is meant to have served as an introduction to the art form of bonsai, there is still much left to learn.

Never be afraid to experiment and try new things and also to learn new things. The world of bonsai can be extremely exciting.

Good luck on your bonsai project and I'm pretty sure this won't be the last!

# Appendix

Here is the bonsai glossary of terms to help you further understand the different terminologies used when growing, cultivating and caring for bonsai plants.

## Bonsai Terminology

### Accent Plant

A small plant that is placed on display along with a bonsai; usually when

a bonsai is being formally displayed at a show or exhibition. It is also sometimes called companion plant.

### Air Layer

A method for growing trees by removing a large branch or

section of trunk from an existing tree to create a new tree.

### Akadama

Refers to a traditional Japanese bonsai soil that is made up of the red volcanic matter of Japan. It has traditionally been used for thousands of years by bonsai artists on many different types of deciduous bonsai trees.

## Apex

Refers to the highest point of a bonsai tree.

## Back budding

Refers to a process of encouraging new growth on a branch where growth is

currently non-existent.

## Broadleaved

Trees which are primarily deciduous and feature broad, flat leaves. These are non-conifer trees.

## Bunjin

A traditional Japanese bonsai style. It is also known as literati. This is a tree that features a tall, slender trunk with foliage only grows near the top.

## Buttress

Refers to the area of a tree trunk where the roots meet the surface of the soil. This is usually styled to imply strength.

## Callus

Refers to the scar tissue that forms over a wound where a branch has been pruned from a tree. The callus is part of the tree's healing process.

## Cambium

Refers to the thin layer of green-colored cell tissue that grows between the bark and the wood of a living tree.

## Canopy

All of the upper-most branches that form the top of a tree.

## Chokkan

A traditional Japanese bonsai style. It is also sometimes known as a formal upright. This is a tree that has an extremely straight trunk with symmetrical branching. It sometimes illustrates strength and order.

## Collected tree

Refers to the process of locating and taking a tree from its natural habitat. This is a tree that has been shaped by the forces of nature alone.

## Conifer

A tree that bears cones. This is primarily evergreen trees such as: pines, cedars, spruces and junipers.

## Cross

Refers to a hybrid that results from cross-fertilization between species or varieties.

## Crown

The upper section of a bonsai where the branches spread out from the

trunk.

## Cultivars

Cultivars are plants that have features desirable to the person growing them. Such characteristics have been deliberately chosen and

can be produced reliably in plants under controlled cultivation.

## Cut-leaved

A bonsai that has leaves which are shaped in very distinct segments.

## Deciduous

Refers to a tree that has a seasonal growth cycle where new foliage is produced in the spring, then grows throughout the summer, turns colors in autumn, and drops in the winter, leaving buds on the branches for next spring's new foliage.

## Defoliation

Refers to the process of removing all leaves to encourage new shoots and possibly smaller leaves.

## Dieback

The death of the tips of branches as a result of extreme weather or possibly disease.

## Divided leaf

A leaf formed of separate sections that emerge from a common base.

## Division

A method of cultivating shrubs by carefully dividing the root ball and

replanting the separated sections.

## Dormant

Refers to the period of the year when there is little or no growth. This usually occurs in late autumn and throughout the winter months.

## Dwarf

A variety or cultivar that is smaller than the species tree, but retains all of

the characteristics of a full size species tree.

## Fertilizer

This is a type of food for trees, shrubs and plants. It is usually comprised of NPK: Nitrogen for the foliage,

Phosphorous for the roots, and Potassium for the flowers.

## Foliage pad

A mass of foliage on a branch. Sometimes known as a cloud.

## Fruit

The part of a plant that carries the seeds; usually berries or fleshy or pod

like.

## Fukinagashi

A traditional Japanese bonsai style. It is also known as windswept. This is a tree that has its trunk and branches swept back in one direction; illustrating a tree exposed to very forceful winds.

## Genus

Refers to a unit of classification for a group of closely related plants.

## Germination

The moment a seed starts to grow, developing roots and shoots.

## Girth

The circumference of the trunk of a tree. It is measured at just above the root

base.

## Grafting

This is a commonly used method for cultivating trees, when cultivation by

seeds or cuttings is impractical or impossible.

## Han-Kengai

A traditional Japanese bonsai style. Also known as semi-cascade. This is where the branches and trunk of a tree are swept down to one side, but not below the top lip of the container. It illustrates a tree subject to violent winds and weather.

## Hardy

A term used to describe trees capable a withstanding winter frost.

## Hokidachi

A traditional Japanese bonsai style. It is also sometimes known as broom. This is where the trunk is semi-circular dome or broom shape.

## Humidity

The amount or degree of moisture in the air.

## Internodal distance

The length of stem between two nodes or leaf joints.

## Ikadabuki

A traditional Japanese bonsai style. Also sometimes known as raft. This is where the tree is laid on its side and its branches are trained vertically and arranged in a group formation.

## Ishitsuki, Ishitzuki

A traditional Japanese bonsai style. It is also sometimes known as root over rock. This is where the tree has its roots arranged so they have grown over and in the crevices of a rock.

## Jin

A branch that has been stripped of its bark and cambium to illustrate a

dead branch. Represents great age or harsh conditions.

## Juvenile foliage

The young leaves of a tree that produces two distinct shapes of leaves; the second type is mature foliage.

## Kabudachi

A traditional Japanese bonsai style. Also sometimes known as clump. This is where the trees' trunks all grow from the same point on the root mass and are more crowded in appearance than a regular group planting.

## Kengai

A traditional Japanese bonsai style. Also sometimes known as cascade. This is where the branches and trunk of the tree are swept to one side and hang below the container. Illustrates a tree on the edge of a mountain cliff subjected to fierce winds.

## Leader

Refers to the main shoot at the top of a tree. This typically indicates the uppermost continuation of the trunk.

## Lime Sulpher

A chemical used to whiten a section of stripped branch or trunk in

order to maintain a jin or shari.

## Loam

A soil mixture comprised of clay, sand and organic matter.

## Mame

A term used in size classification of bonsai trees. The smallest is bonsai.

## Moyogi

A traditional Japanese bonsai style. Also sometimes known as informal upright. This is where the trunk curves through its taper up to the apex.

## Nebari

The exposed surface roots of a bonsai.

Needle

A type of leaf that is narrow and often has a stiff texture.

## New wood

A stem or twig on a bonsai that originated during the present season's

growth.

## Nitrogen

An essential element of plant nutrition. It is identified by the chemical symbol N. Important for growth of stems and leaves.

## Node

The point on a trunk or branch where the leaf buds emerge.

## Old wood

A stem or twig on a bonsai that originated during the prior season's

growth.

## Peat

Refers to organic matter that is partially decomposed. When it is used as an ingredient of potting soil it helps in moisture retention.

## Perlite

A form of volcanic rock that is heat-treated to develop a lightweight, coarse

granule. When it is used as a component of potting soil it offers advantages in ventilation and water retention properties.

## Phosphorous

Another essential element of plant nutrition. It is identified by the chemical

symbol P. It assists in development of roots, ripening of fruits and seeds.

## Pinching

A technique used in bonsai cultivation of controlling and shaping the

growth of foliage by pulling off soft new shoots with the finger and thumb

in a pinching motion.

## Potassium

This is the third essential element of plant nutrition. It is identified by the chemical symbol K. It promotes strong new growth, development of flower buds and fruit formation.

## Pot-bound

Refers to the state of a container grown plant where the root growth has

filled the container to the point of eliminating all vital air spaces.

## Prostrate

The characteristic growth habit of a plant that naturally tends to grow

along the ground instead of upright.

## Pruning

The process of controlling the shape and growth rate of a tree by cutting

back the shoots, stems and branches.

## Raceme

A type of elongated flower that is composed of individual stalks all growing

from a central stem. Wisteria is an example.

## Ramification

Refers to the dense branching structure of a bonsai that only develops after years of repeated pruning of the branches.

## Repotting

The process of replanting a bonsai tree at regular intervals to perform

health maintaining tasks such as: root washing, inspecting, soil refreshing, pruning and potting in a different pot.

## Rootball

Refers to the large mass of roots and soil that are visible when a tree is taken out of its pot or pulled from the ground.

## Root pruning

The practice of cutting back the roots of bonsai to provide space in

the container for fresh soil and to encourage new root growth.

## Rootstock

The root system and main stem to be used as the base of a new tree

when cultivating through the grafting process.

## Scion

A small section of a tree, which contains all of the desirable characteristics

of the parent tree that will be cultivated into a new tree through the grafting

process.

## Shakan

A traditional Japanese bonsai style. Also sometimes known as slanting. This is where the trees' trunk, appears similar to the formal upright style, but the trunk is slanting to one side.

## Shari

Refers to an area where the bark and cambium have been removed from the trunk to illustrate the struggle against fierce weather.

## Species

The unit of classification for a plant with identifiable characteristics.

## Suiseki

Stones that appear to resemble large boulders or mountains and illustrate the spirit or essence of each. This is sometime used in a formal bonsai display.

## Taproot

The large root of a tree that grows vertically downward, anchoring it into

the ground. It is typically referred to in bonsai due to its need to be

pruned shorter or removed for container cultivation.

## Tokonoma

A Japanese tradition of creating a specific area in the home where bonsai,

accessory plants, Suiseki, and scrolls are displayed together in harmony.

## Wound sealant

A number of compounds formulated to seal cuts made on branches or the

trunk of a bonsai tree to prevent the loss of moisture and promote healing.

## Yamadori

Refers to trees that are collected from the wild and have been shaped by only nature and have been collected to be developed into bonsai.

## Yose-ue

A traditional Japanese bonsai style. Also sometimes known as a group or forest. This is where the trees are arranged in a container to resemble a group or forest of trees.

Now you can feel like an expert bonsai grower!

ISBN-13: 978-1482779370

Printed in the United States of America

Made in the USA
San Bernardino, CA
27 June 2016